En parejas 1

ESTUDIANTE B

Actividad 1: La inscripción

Fill out the following card with information about yourself.

Primer apellido

Segundo apellido

Nombre

Edad

Ciudad natal

Estado

Número de teléfono

En caso de emergencia llamar a:

Primer apellido

Segundo apellido

Nombre

Número de teléfono

Parentesco: _____ Padre   _____ Madre

_____ Otro/a   (especifique relación _____)

You are registering for classes. Your partner, who works at the registration desk, will ask you a series of questions based on the preceding information. Your partner will begin. When your partner has finished, reverse roles and fill out the card below with information from your partner.

Primer apellido

Segundo apellido

Nombre

Edad

Ciudad natal

Estado

Número de teléfono

En caso de emergencia llamar a:

Primer apellido

Segundo apellido

Nombre

Número de teléfono

Parentesco: _____ Padre _____ Madre

_____ Otro/a (especifique relación _____)

Actividad 2: Información, buenos días

You are the directory assistance operator. Your duties include giving out telephone numbers and addresses. Some useful phrases are:

¿Cómo se escribe . . . ?
¿Sabe Ud. el segundo apellido / la dirección?

You begin by saying: *Información, buenos días.*

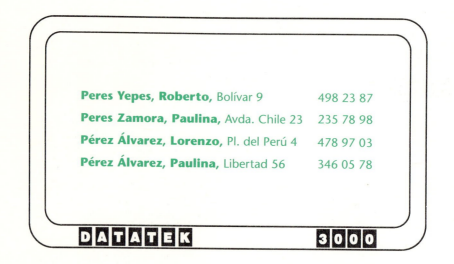

Peres Yepes, Roberto, Bolívar 9   498 23 87

Peres Zamora, Paulina, Avda. Chile 23   235 78 98

Pérez Álvarez, Lorenzo, Pl. del Perú 4   478 97 03

Pérez Álvarez, Paulina, Libertad 56   346 05 78

DATATEK   3000

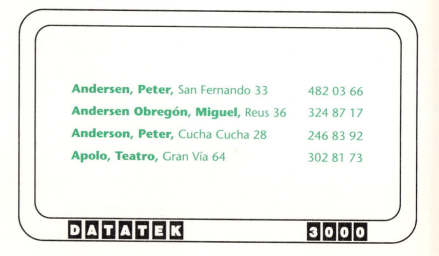

Andersen, Peter, San Fernando 33   482 03 66

Andersen Obregón, Miguel, Reus 36   324 87 17

Anderson, Peter, Cucha Cucha 28   246 83 92

Apolo, Teatro, Gran Vía 64   302 81 73

DATATEK   3000

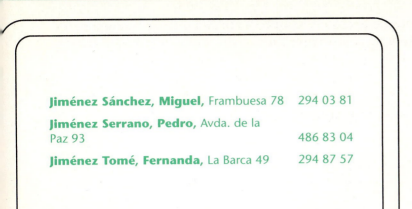

Jiménez Sánchez, Miguel, Frambuesa 78   294 03 81

Jiménez Serrano, Pedro, Avda. de la
Paz 93   486 83 04

Jiménez Tomé, Fernanda, La Barca 49   294 87 57

DATATEK 3000

Domínguez Torres, Rafael, Viriato 56   449 57 93

Domínguez Trujillo, Matilde, Lagasca 16   228 44 72

Domínguez Turrión, Bibiana, Ibiza 64   235 83 71

Domínguez Turrión, Viviana, Menorca 3   275 74 66

DATATEK 3000

Giménez Urquijo, José, Ballesta 5   492 77 39

Giménez Vicens, Marta, Matute 23   294 79 40

Giménez Viñolas, Miguel, Lope de
Rueda 10   395 73 06

Giménez Zapata, Miguel, Conde
Duque 32   473 78 25

DATATEK 3000

You work for an international exchange program in Madrid and are arranging for a number of American students to be picked up at the train station. This is the information you were given from your boss:

Kurt Childs	Zamora	10:00
Adrian Dorschel	Santiago	1:00
Becky Weber	León	10:30
Jeanie Voss	Salamanca	9:45
Heath Mueller	Oviedo	12:00
Kara Straka	Vigo	1:40

You know that your information isn't always accurate and there may be delays, so you are calling the train station for the most current information about arrival times and platform numbers. The following questions may be useful to help get the information you need:

¿Me puede decir . . . ?
¿Sabe Ud. a qué hora llega . . . ?
¿Hay retraso?
¿A qué andén llega . . . ?

Your partner will begin.

	Hora	Andén
Kurt Childs		
Adrian Dorschel		
Becky Weber		
Jeanie Voss		
Heath Mueller		
Kara Straka		

You work at the information desk at the airport in Caracas. Look at the following departure board on your computer screen and give the appropriate information. Phrases that may be useful include:

¿Cuál es el número de vuelo?
¿En qué línea?
Sale a las . . .
Sale de la puerta número . . .
No sé, no hay información.

You begin by answering the phone and saying: *Aeropuerto Maiquetía, buenos días.*

S	A	L	I	D	A	S

Nº de Vuelo		Destino	Hora	Puerta
Avianca	345	Bogotá		
Avianca	582	Cartagena	13:15	6
Iberia	465	Madrid	Retraso	10
Pan Am	632	San Juan / Miami	Retraso 8:35	3
Lan Chile	301	Santiago	9:15	7
Lan Chile	420	Lima / Santiago	14:35	22
Lacsa	203	San José	Retraso 10:00	11

Actividad 5: El tiempo de mañana

Ask your partner questions to complete the following weather map for Argentina. Exchange information. Use expressions such as:

> **¿Qué tiempo va a hacer mañana en . . . ?**
> **Mañana va a hacer . . .**
> **Va a estar . . .**
> **Va a . . .**
> **Va a hacer . . . grados.**

Your partner will begin.

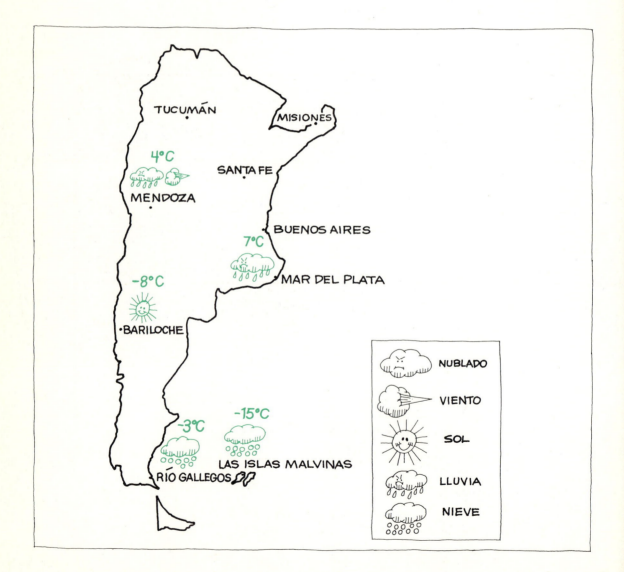

Your friend wants to go with you to the movies this week. Discuss your work schedule with your friend and decide what film you would like to see. Use the following partial list of movies in your city and your work schedule to help you make your decision. Useful expressions include:

¿Qué vas a hacer el martes?
¿Tienes planes para el jueves?
¿Estás libre el miércoles?
¿Quieres ver . . . ?

No me gustan . . .
Tengo que . . .
¿A qué hora . . . ?
No puedo, necesito . . .

Your partner will begin.

CARTELERA PARA ESTA SEMANA

ALFAVILLE
Superman V, aventura, todas las edades. 5:15, 7:15, 9:15, 11:15.

APOLO
E.T. regresa a casa, ciencia ficción, todas las edades. 5:00, 7:10, 9:20, 11:30.

GROUCHO
Viaje a las estrellas VII, ciencia ficción, mayores de 13 años. 5:00, 7:05, 9:10, 11:15.

LUNA: SALA 1
Muerte en el Expreso Oriente, misterio, mayores de 18 años. 5:10, 7:14, 9:18, 11:22.

LUNA: SALA 2
La Bamba, biografía, mayores de 18 años. 5:00, 7:02, 9:04, 11:06.

Horario de trabajo

lunes: *libre*

martes: *3:00 pm a 8:30 pm*

miércoles: *libre*

jueves: *3:00 pm a 8:30 pm*

viernes: *3:00 pm a 8:30 pm*

sábado: *libre*

domingo: *2:00 pm a 10:00 pm*

Actividad 7: La agenda

Your business partner is calling you to get your schedule for the week. The two of you have just started a company that distributes sports equipment. You are trying to mix business with pleasure, but you don't really want your partner to know that. The following is a list of things that you are going to do this week. Use expressions such as:

Tengo que . . .

Voy a . . .

You begin by answering the phone and saying: *¿Aló?*

lunes:	11:00 hablar con el abogado 4:10 viajar a Valdivia en tren
martes:	trabajar con Jorge Ramírez (director del Club Vidasana) por la mañana, comer con Pablo Camacho (un amigo), 5:30 regresar a Santiago en tren
miércoles:	ir a Viña del Mar, visitar la compañía C.A. CH. (Club Atlético de Chile), ir al campo de golf con un amigo, regresar a Santiago por la tarde
jueves:	9:00 hablar con el abogado de la compañía, trabajar en la oficina, ir a Valparaíso por la tarde
viernes:	hablar con el director de I.B.M. por la mañana, ver un partido de fútbol con mi padre
sábado:	visitar a mis padres en Valparaíso
domingo:	regresar a Santiago por la noche

Actividad 8: El accidente

You work at the bus station in Santa Marta, Colombia. There have been problems with the loudspeaker system and it is impossible to page people. You will try to locate people, but only if it is an emergency. Use phrases like:

El altavoz no funciona, necesito una descripción de las personas.
¿Cómo son?
¿Qué llevan?
¿Es alto/a . . . ?
¡Ah, sí! Ahora sé quiénes son.
¿Lleva una falda blanca o negra?

You begin by answering the phone and saying:

Estación de autobuses, a sus órdenes.

This is the view of the station from your window:

Actividad 9: ¿Quién es?

Think of a well-known living or fictitious person that your partner will know. Your partner will try to determine who it is by asking you questions. Answer your partner's questions by responding **sí** or **no**. Do not offer any extra information. When your partner has guessed the identity, switch roles and guess one of the people on your partner's list. Here is a list of famous people for your partner to guess:

1. Whoopie Goldberg
2. Billy Crystal
3. Ted Kennedy
4. Martina Navratilova
5. Dan Marino
6. Barbara Walters
7. ???

You may want to make a game of this by awarding a point for each question asked. The person who determines the correct identities while asking the least number of questions is the winner.

Your partner will begin.

Actividad 10: La universidad

You are at the Universidad Cristóbal Colón and you need to find out the location of the following places: **la biblioteca, la facultad de psicología, la cafetería, la piscina olímpica**. Ask your partner questions such as:

¿Sabes dónde está . . . ?
¿La biblioteca está . . . ?

You begin by saying: *¿Sabes dónde está . . . ?*

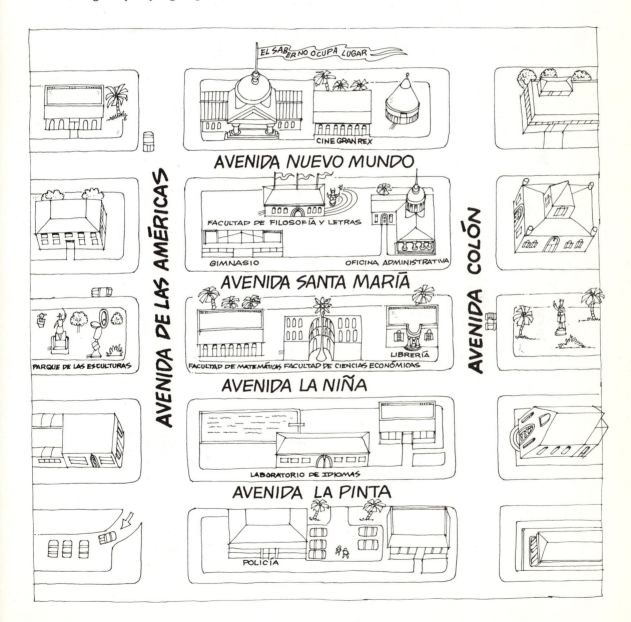

You and your partner have a similar but somewhat different drawing. There are seven differences between them. Describe your picture and ask questions about your partner's picture to find out what the differences are.

Your partner will begin.

The following crossword puzzle is on clothing and parts of the body. You have the horizontal words and your partner has the vertical ones. You need to give clues **(pistas)** to your partner. Use phrases like the following:

> **Es generalmente de . . .**
> **Esta parte del cuerpo está en . . .**
> **Es para . . .**

When you are finished, your partner will ask you for clues about the horizontal words.

You begin by saying: *¿Qué es la uno vertical?*

Actividad 13:   Se perdió . . .

You are the manager of a department store. A customer comes to see you because he/she has lost someone. Interview the customer and draw the person who is lost. You may need to ask questions like:

> **¿Tiene pelo rubio / largo / corto . . . ?**
> **¿Lleva falda / vestido / etc.?**

Your partner will begin.

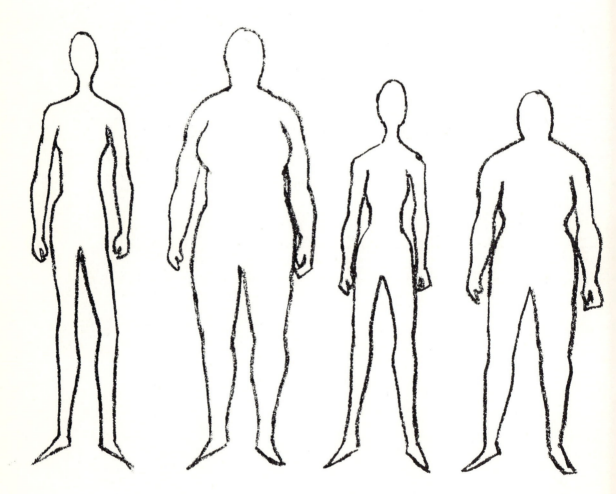

Actividad 14:   Si te doy esto . . .

You have an identical twin sister who lives in Tierra Del Fuego, Argentina, where it is always cold. You live in Salta, Argentina, where it is very hot. You will be taking a ski trip to Portillo, Chile, to enjoy the mountains. Make a list of what you think you will need. Your sister is going to call you so ask her if you can borrow some clothes. In the past you have always lent each other clothes, but neither of you ever gives the other anything without getting something in return.

Use phrases like: **Voy a ir a . . .**   **Me gustaría tener . . .**
                    Necesito . . .   **Si me das . . . te doy . . .**

Other vocabulary that may be helpful: **de rayas**   **de lunares**   **de cuadros**

You begin by saying: *¿Aló?*

This is your family tree (you are the person circled in black). Your partner will ask you questions about your family to try to reproduce your entire family tree. Don't volunteer any information that is not specifically asked of you. When your partner is finished, ask him/her questions to reproduce his/her family tree. You need to find out all of the members' names, occupations, and ages. Ask very specific questions such as:

¿Tienes hermanos?   **¿Qué hace él?**
¿Cómo se llama tu tío?   **¿Cuántos años tiene . . . ?**

Your partner will begin.

Silvestre Estalón Días, dentista, 87 años

MARTA VIÑOLAS

Rufina Tamaya, secretaria, 45 años

Paco, ingeniero, 56 años

Silvia, economista, 58 años

Daniel Olivas Viña, policía, 54 años

Marta, agente de viajes, 24 años

Cris, bióloga, 25 años

Darío, enfermero, 30 años

Ana Mansio Sot[o] profesora, 28 añ[os]

Jorgito

Actividad 16:   El catálogo

You work taking orders by phone for Tienda Los Gallegos in Puerto Rico. You are very unhappy with your job because your boss is a stickler for detail—one mistake in the order and you have to pay for the item being purchased. So you must double check every piece of information that is given to you, to be sure it is accurate. Answer the phone and take an order, filling out the following order form.

You begin by saying: **Tienda Los Gallegos, buenos días.**

---

t i e n d a ■ l o s ■ g a l l e g o s

Avenida Patricio 38   Caparra, P. R. 00920   (809) 798–6549

Nombre y apellido: _____

Dirección: _____

Ciudad: _____

Teléfono: _____

Tarjeta de crédito: ____ Visa   ____ Mastercard   ____ American Express

Número de tarjeta: □□□□ □□□□ □□□□ □□□□

Artículo	Talla	Color	Cantidad	Precio
			TOTAL $	

Actividad 17:   ¿Es igual o diferente?

You have to describe to your partner the even-numbered objects on your list without actually saying the word. Your partner will describe to you the odd-numbered objects. On hearing your partner's descriptions, you have to decide if he/she is describing the same object you have under the same number.

Your partner will begin.

		Iguales	Diferentes			Iguales	Diferentes
1.	diccionario	___	___	6.	jabón	___	___
2.	cuchara	___	___	7.	disco compacto	___	___
3.	sombrero	___	___	8.	flash	___	___
4.	maleta	___	___	9.	tenedor	___	___
5.	sofá	___	___	10.	película	___	___

Actividad 18: El mensaje telefónico

Your name is Mariano Mores and you call Mrs. Rey, your travel agent, to tell her that you want to make a reservation for the trip for two to Mexico she offered you last week ($150 per person per week). You want to leave on a Monday evening and come back on a Sunday.

Your partner will begin.

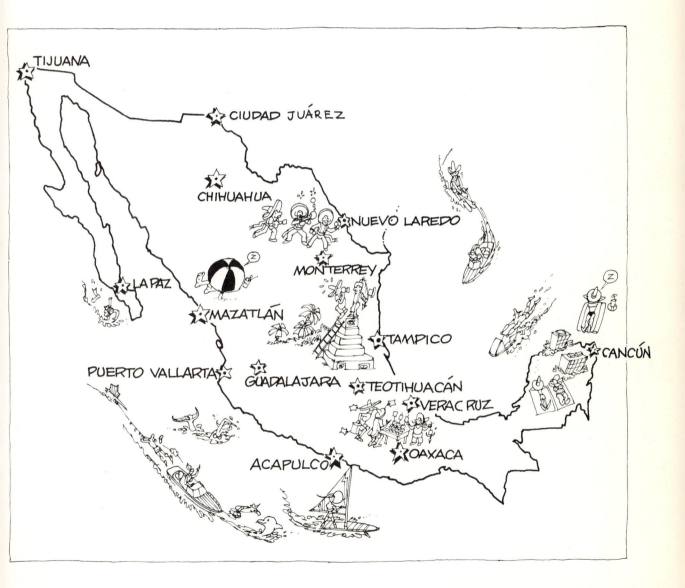

Actividad 19: ¿Quién vive en qué piso?

Look at the drawing of the student residence below. Share your clues **(pistas)** with your partner to complete the chart on the next page. Here are some useful expressions:

¿Puedes repetir, por favor?   **¿Dónde vive . . . ?**
No entiendo.   **¿Qué estudia . . . ?**

You begin by reading the first clue.

1. La chica que vive en el último piso es de Venezuela.
2. El estudiante de matemáticas es de Colombia.
3. Silvana Caycedo, que es estudiante de medicina, vive justo debajo del chico de Bolivia.
4. Gustavo Gutiérrez, estudiante de economía, vive entre Tomás Schaeffer y Mariana Suárez.
5. La persona del 4ºA estudia teatro.
6. Pablo Morales vive en el último piso en el apartamento B y estudia biología.
7. Sonia Rodríguez, uruguaya, vive en el 1ºB.
8. Mariana Suárez, de Perú, vive al lado del estudiante argentino que estudia guitarra.
9. La estudiante de computación es de Nicaragua.
10. El estudiante de economía es de Madrid.

Nombre	Nacionalidad	Estudiante de . . .	Apartamento

The following pictures are part of a story and, except for the first one, they are out of order. Your partner also has drawings that are part of this story. Ask your partner about the missing drawings to find out the order in which the events happened. When you finish putting the drawings in order, give the story a title. Use expressions such as:

¿Qué ocurrió después?
¿Tienes un dibujo de la chica en su casa?

Your partner will begin.

Actividad 21:   ¿Qué más necesitamos?

You and your friend are planning a meal for tonight at your place. Each of you has a recipe as well as a picture with some ingredients that you have at home. Find out what ingredients neither of you have, so that your friend can buy them on the way to your house.

You begin by saying: *¿Qué necesitamos para la cena de esta noche?*

Sopa de frijoles negros

2 tazas y media de frijoles negros
6 tazas de agua
4 tazas de caldo de verduras
2 cucharadas de aceite de oliva
1 cebolla
4 dientes de ajo
1 cucharadita de orégano
1 cucharadita de comino

Lavar los frijoles y luego ponerlos en una cacerola con agua. Hervir. Luego cocinar a fuego lento hasta que los frijoles absorban casi toda el agua (30 a 40 minutos). Añadir el caldo. Mientras tanto, cocinar en una sartén la cebolla, el ajo, el comino y el orégano en el aceite. Añadir sal si es necesario. Luego añadir esta mezcla a los frijoles. Servir bien caliente.

Actividad 22: ¿Lo hizo?

You and your roommate are having a party tonight at your apartment. Your roommate's mother has been visiting and has been doing the cleaning. Your roommate is out running errands and he/she calls you to check on what his/her mother has done. Ask your roommate if he/she has done the things he/she was supposed to do.

You begin by answering the phone: *¿Aló?*

Lista de cosas para hacer en el apartamento
- lavar los platos
- limpiar la alfombra de la sala
- limpiar el baño
- ponerles agua a las plantas
- bañar el perro

Cosas que va a hacer mi compañero/a:
- pagar el gas
- comprar comida para el perro
- comprar Coca-Cola
- pagar el teléfono

Actividad 23:   Hispanos famosos

Complete this chart about famous Hispanics by asking your partner questions. Make sure to use the preterit when exchanging information.

Your partner will begin.

	FECHA	NACIONALIDAD	OCUPACIÓN	ALGO IMPORTANTE
Frida Kahlo	1907 – ?	mexicana	pintora	casarse con Diego Rivera
Salvador Allende	? – 1973	chileno	político, presidente de Chile, médico	
Pablo Casals		español	violoncelista, director de orquesta	
Alfonsina Storni		argentina	poetisa	defender los derechos de la mujer
Emiliano Zapata	1883 – ?	mexicano	político revolucionario	participar en la revolución de 1910
Isabel la Católica	1451 – 1504	española	reina	financiar el viaje de Colón
José Martí	? – 1895	cubano	poeta, escritor, abogado	
Carlos Gardel		argentino	cantante, compositor	hacer el tango famoso
Violeta Parra	1918 – 1967	chilena	cantante, compositora	
Roberto Clemente	1934 – 1972	puertorriqueño	jugador de béisbol	

Actividad 24: Las últimas vacaciones

Your partner is going to ask you questions about the last vacation you took. Base your answers on these pages from your scrapbook.

	Fecha de salida	Hora de salida	Hora de llegada
Santiago/ Chile	16/12	3:59 AM	11:45 PM
Portillo	17/12	12:00 AM	2:00 AM

Hostería del Estudiante
Portillo, Chile

Habitación doble

5 noches $15.000

EL CHILENO

comida típica

Edelweiss
Restaurante
alemán

When your partner is finished, ask about his/her last vacation. Ask specific questions. Try to use all of the following question words and phrases.

¿Adónde . . . ?   ¿Por qué . . . ?
¿Cuándo . . . ?   ¿Cuánto dinero . . . ?
¿Con quién . . . ?   ¿En qué hotel . . . ?
¿Cuánto tiempo . . . ?   ¿En qué restaurantes . . . ?
¿Qué . . . ?   ¿Qué souvenirs . . . ?

After discussing your vacations, plan a trip together, taking into consideration each other's likes and dislikes. Use phrases such as:

Me gustaría . . .   Tenemos que ir a . . .
Podemos ir a . . .   No quiero . . .
Debemos visitar . . .   ¿Por qué no vamos a . . . ?

Actividad 25:   Amigos

By this time you should know most of the people in your Spanish class quite well. Write a description of one of your classmates on the card below. It should be a minimum of ten lines. Make sure your clues go from general characteristics to more specific ones. Your partner will read you a description of someone and you should try to guess who it is. When you are finished, read your description to your partner to see if he/she can guess who it is. Use phrases such as:

Es una persona alta / baja / delgada / etc.
Tiene pelo . . .
Tiene . . . hermanos / años.
Le gusta . . .
Vive en . . .
Juega al . . .

Your partner will begin.

NOTAS NOTAS NOTAS NOTAS NOTAS NOTAS NOTAS NOTAS NOTAS